HOMEBODY
STAINS

NEHA ANN

Contents

Homebody Stains   *vii*

Acknowledgements   *ix*

1. Home   1

2. Soft (tw: Self Harm)   2

3. Paints   5

4. Citylights   7

—

5. Language   13

6. Chapter   15

7. Secrets   17

8. Untitled   21

—

9. Hands (tw: Suicide)   27

10. Hopes   29

11. Human   31

12. Fear   33

13. Letters   35

—

14. Warnings   39

15. Homebody Stains   41

16. Metaphors For The Night   43

17. Bedspread   45

—

18. Fossils   49

Contents

19. Family Ties   52

20. Uncovered Hangovers   54

21. Cuckoos   60

—

22. Shadow   65

23. Beast   67

24. Empty   69

25. Catharsis   72

26. Clarity   75

—

27. Letter Writing   79

28. Story For Santa   83

29. Tales   85

30. Comfort   88

—

31. Reasons   93

32. Guilt   96

33. Rants   98

—

34. Monsters   103

35. Pages From My Thought   105

36. Tears (tw: Death)   108

37. Drought   110

—

Contents

38. Fragmented Memory   119

39. Imaginations   122

40. Warmth   125

41. Love   127

—

About The Author   133

A Note From Neha   135

Homebody Stains

Neha Ann's debut book "Homebody stains" is a collection of poetry that allows the reader to experience life through their grey eyes. A search for finding their home in themselves and how the memories have tainted their body, leaving stains wherever they go.

To see more content through their eyes, @griefwithbenefits

Acknowledgements

I have some control on determining what and who I am but I will not be able to deny the impact these people have had on me. So, this is for y'all. Gratitude would be an understatement for all that you have done and I hope you know how much you mean to me.

Ma, who has been my support system and the biggest cheerleader I could ever ask for. Remember it is us against the world. Always. My grandparents (Ammachi, Appacha, Ammumma and Appuppan) even though we have our ups and downs, has always believed in me. All the art, music, poems and stories exist because you believed. My uncles and aunt (Manuacha, Sunitha Aunty and Joe Uncle) whose adoration and attempts at pushing me out of my comfort zones have resulted in this book. Sucheta ma'am is the first person to read anything I have ever written and my constant. Thank you, for being my partner in crime for almost everything . I would not be here alive if it were not for BTS and SHINee who made life a little better, promised to stay and have not let go of my hand ever since. Salvia,Gayathri, Swathi, Cristina Yang, Yellow Tulip, Lily and Yoongles - thank you for staying and for always being the sunsets in my life. Biru, my publisher and a creative genius, for turning my words into something so beautiful. You deserve it all. I could not thank everyone I had in mind but know that I am forever grateful to you.

Bangalore, Salvia and Chai, I dedicate this book to you.

Welcome to the Magic Shop.

1. Home

At 8,
Home for me was a box of KitKats
That uncle got me every Christmas
home for me was the very thought of
Stealing them at night with pa
And munching on them while
We watched reruns of his favourite tv show.

At 15
Home for me was a brown-eyed boy,
Who claimed to conquer the galaxies
That lay undisturbed in my eyes.
Home for me was the lazy morning hugs
and the toast with chai routines that
he made every evening.

At 21,
Home for me is a box of empty letters
And a year-old wine,
Home for me is a heart
that you've left behind watching sunflowers
bloom slowly in winter.

2. Soft (TW: self harm)

I break things that seem,
Soft.
Like your
dried up lips,
and your sultry
heart.
My pixelated fingers,
pinning for your
naked shadow,
that shut down the quiet
mumbling,
of the sunlight.
My house,
is the runway,
for all departing souls.
Fictional yet,
betrayed at your last breath.
Maybe, the stories we wrote
were just scraped knives
and moulded lies.

The wooden shelf
cares less for my glances,

I hear it
whispering to
the ruined chair
behind,
how the girl in pink
once laid
on the scorching
fields of utilised artefacts.
I tore away,
every one of the letters,
I had scratched
on those unsanitary journals.

You holler in your sleep.
murmuring,
roughly about,
those lilies that hugged my eyelids,
my eldritch obsession with
the smell of
freshly baked loaves of bread,
the stance of my thumb
when I laugh.
I look up from my half-written poem.
I find your wrinkles smirk,
at your secret attachment.
Bundling up my blades,
I rush back to the bottle of Chivas.

I break things that seem,

soft.

Like you and my overflowing veins.

3. Paints

I hear him every day.
Sinking to the marble.
I wake up every time the light turns on.
Bit of a stalker, I am.
Obsessed with your work.
You rush off when the clock strikes 7.
Are you a lover?
Or a mere catapult?

I walk by your house,
Your mother looks down
at the breakfast she set for you.
Mumbles a word or two.
Your father never came home.
Was he tired of seeking you out?

You enjoyed your girls,
Like how I enjoy my poems.
Exotic and fulfilling.
I hear them scream your name.
Was it your name?

What do you do when it gets dark?

Are you afraid of the willows outside?
Or are you too exhausted to utter your fear?
I have seen you pacing at 2 AM.
Was it a lover's corner with the Moon, herself?
Or were you expecting someone?

I heard you cry on the night you finally smiled.
I could hear the metal sharpening against your table.
Was it for yourself?
Or for the lady who made you sweat?
You didn't gorge on your dinner.
You were waiting for someone.
I could sense you walking to the marble tiles again.

This time you aren't alone.
I strive to see your companion for today.
Yet, I only hear a sigh.
You left.
You were alone, you said.
I was there.
Walking, holding your hand.
At least in my thoughts.
I push myself to cry for you.
Guilt was all I could feel.
This was a part of me that could move.
So, I don't know who died today.
Me or the neighbour who painted his body red.

4. Citylights

I wake up to the racing August rain patterns on my window.

I look over at his misshapen body,

failing to string along any words for his void smile.

His name was Firoz, he made the fluffiest pancakes

and left cigars half burnt,

a little over thirty,

binocular eyes and walked with a limp.

We danced the previous night,

stopping only to ask if the other was tired.

The next few hours were a blur, slow dancing to the
intoxicating air that mused around the city.

I smiled a little, watching his sculpted fingers play with my
hair

and climbed all the nine clouds

when we kissed after the frozen kulfis from Prem Chacha's
shop.

He said he liked the way I tasted

as if Kulfi was suddenly a person.

Friday nights were spent at the thrift bookstore

or on a late-night movie date, which always ended in a kadak
chai and momos.

Promises and kulfis from Chachas always made every fight less
illusionary.

I stood at the departure,
with October winds brushing past my numb broken figure,
waving to him 'good luck' as
he made his way to another country,
no better than mine.
Kadak chai was soon replaced
with tequila shots and Marlboro puffs.

The feeling that battered my frightening soul
soon fell for a man with Kafka's smirk.
He left every morning
before I woke up, leaving the sheets folded.
Thanking me for a service I did not know about.
He showed me off at parties like a consolation prize,
touching me as though I was a burning stove.
I took him to Chacha's shop for Pista Kulfi
and watched him eat it.
He was sloppy
and boasted that
his place had better ones.
We went back home,
he kissed my frozen lips with hunger
and pushed me away all of a sudden,
saying I disgust him with that horrible taste of kulfi.

I wrote a letter every time I made love to him

and threw it among my other unsent ones in the drawer.

I whispered into his ears later that night

and eloped with the dead sky.

I walked in search of a home that painted my body with rain

patterns.

I walked in search of a heart that beat irrationally every time I

whispered poetry.

I walked in search of a city that never sighed.

Healing (verb) : /hiːl/

become sound or healthy again; alleviate (a person's distress or anguish); correct or put right (an undesirable situation).

5. Language

When I first cried to my friend about the man I love.
She called me immature and walked away.
That same day, I told my mother about the way he looks at
me.
She shut herself in the puja room,
praying to the 'undiscriminating' above to show me wisdom.
So, I wrote to the man I love
about the fantasies that we would live through soon.
I wrote to the man I love
about the labels that tighten around my neck
and the detachment of belonging.
The man I love wrote back in just a few lines.
He said I was dangerous.
And his mother always told him not to play with fire
or talk to figures that spoke a language
he did not know.
He wrote back the second time,
telling me how incapable I was to take care of myself.
Now, this started a war.
More gruesome than both the world wars combined.
I finally replied,
failing at words but ending the note with bloodshed.

The man I love,

travelled 81 km to bid farewell to the Berlin Wall,

which I had torn apart.

I cried out to my mother about the way he struck me.

She watched as I held onto the tip of the saree.

The man I love never told me

he loved me.

6 years later,

I sit by the cafe feverishly gushing past the pages of the book

I finally stole.

I see a familiar face.

A gutless smile.

The man I loved went on to tell me

how I started speaking a language he knew.

while pointing to the book I am reading.

I laugh while watching his face wrinkle into a black hole.

The figure he now loves had always spoken

the tongue of the Devil.

6. Chapter

- (i) I wonder what life would be like when

all the poetry slips out from your wide hips.

The witches and the classy slayers of the wondrous years whisper the challenges.

I've seen buttons rush off your shirts

to caress your lap as if it would die otherwise.

Yet, I wonder what life would be

if we weren't the epitome of this wretched beauty of platonic destruction.

I wonder what love would be

if all the glances we made stayed true to us.

I grow old with every breath I take.

Feeling this October sun burning through your tangled hair.

You scream Post Malone lyrics out loud at dawn.

You don't wonder what is left

of the smitten pillows and the drowning hugs.

You believe that

you'll never fall into the depth

yet stop at the brim to pull me up.

It wouldn't take months to erase,

a shot of Old Monk and a crushed clove mix should be the

remedy.

Staircases and stolen grips,

you've made a home in these static elements.

This is the cold month of forbidden love.

- (ii) She has her mother's eyes and her father's mouth.

A story that was taken away by the witches of rust.

She could hear her ancestors' breath down her spine.

She has poetry on her bones and scars in her smiles.

A warrior in disguise for a prophecy that snided her.

She has her mother's eyes and her father's mouth.

A tongue that shed Latin and Greek.

She walked around like she owned the place.

Swords like smiles and faces that changed colours.

The gown was pasted with wilted flowers.

She has her mother's eyes and her father's mouth.

She breaks her heart every day like the wind chimes in a locked-up house.

This is for the times we could see the stars crying in a clear sky.

7. Secrets

I lay on the,

freshly mowed grass.

My head on your lap and

Kafka in my hands.

You tell me all your secrets,

that seemed like,

magic pop just bursting on my tongue.

The old monk was getting too comfortable for you.

So that day.

You chose to chase the clouds.

You came back,

to my room

at 4 AM,

with the fragrance of,

Givenchy Eau de Givenchy.

Slowly,

getting into bed.

Your hands finding their way,

down my thighs and

slightly feeling me.

I tell you,

I wasn't in a mood.

You back off.

You, talk to me in that,
husky slow tone
that you know,
I cannot resist.
And there we were,
1 hour later,
just panting.
If you felt like you needed me, now.
Your body hugged me in ways,
only my hands knew how.
Your breath gracefully
matched mine.

This was the 4th time,
and I was into you,
'This is special.'
Was your only answer every time
I asked you,
What we were.
You tell me not to seek a future in you.

I was your Qudisa Begum.
Unnoticed.
I nod, suddenly covering myself.
Ashamed.
Three days later,

We were fighting over Platonic relations,

when you said, you love me.

You wanted to win the argument.

I knew this trick.

Yet, you kept going back.

I believed it.

We rushed back to my room.

This time, I let you do it over and over.

This was special,

I was yours.

I heard your groan,

I felt disgusted.

Not special.

Just filled with remorse.

It was fast like you were in a hurry.

Did you have somewhere to be?

I hear you tiptoeing out at 6.

I rub my eyes,

to see your sculpted body just walking away.

I miss the freshly mowed grass,

Kafka stopped brushing past my fingers.

My room has got a lock now.

It's been four years,

Since I heard the familiar knock.

And now,

I stand at your wedding,

listen to you,

say your vows,

ending it with,

I love you, repeatedly.

Not to me.

Only this time,

It was to Mumtaz.

8. Untitled

It was not crazy for the lady who killed herself 57 years ago.
Yet, they found it delusional
when they found scars all over my sepia body.
Theo cannot eat properly cause
his brother's bloody ear comes to his mind.
the man who had a peculiar taste for gory death
became a feast to the coyotes in the 1960s's
you laughed at him
when he threatened to kill himself with an oyster knife.
You mocked him,
told him to give you the pearls before he died.
they tell you not to crumble to non-existence.
they grave poems
and paint with their fascinating colours.
they tell you to breathe,
while they shoot themselves at the mere age of 37.
I look up to these people.
they left back suicide notes in every poem that they had
scribbled on.
they were artists
who kept silver blades hidden under the words.
They bleed moonlight.
But, that's another poem for the sky to write.

18:54 Day 13

She wants to be all the metaphors of the lilac sky that she writes about.

I am the sky.

The one where you feel as though the clouds are too soft

Or

The rain that falls is salty and raw.

You complain about the bats that live in my hair,

You say you cannot sleep.

Neither can I.

But the dark circles never show up.

You water the Bonsai every day,

Yet, you never stopped to look at me.

Why?

Am I that bright that I redecorate your scars?

Yesterday, the man who sat behind the sun craved my body.

Said that even godly beings have needs.

That same evening,

I burnt into a bright orange while the clouds ran to cover me.

On my run,

I see you stare at his picture while taking a long drag.

I've been hiding for centuries now.

You never came in search.

The man painted my once lilac body into a maroon shadow.

I stay with him now.

But I still send the bats

to your bed hoping to see the blueish red flecks in your eyes.

—

Growth (noun) : /grəʊθ/

The process of developing physically, mentally, or spiritually.

9. Hands (TW: suicide)

I scream out that it isn't his hands on my throat.

I not know whose.

It's gripping tight on my voice that once

screamed out Jeans' words.

My hands are pitch black colour.

I recognise them from the time,

I murdered your lips.

The same touch.

I see it now.

My hands are around my neck.

They want me to choke

and not to die,

but to know the pain of dying.

The final struggle for a breath.

They are around

when I write letters to everyone except you.

Letters that are later found crumbled outside my door.

The same pitch-black marks.

I grew up on a farm, you see.

Where families hushed about their sons' going on playdates
with melancholy.

I was told not to tell my stories of escaping death.
Haha.

That's what they called it.
You see, I was not a lady two aeons ago.
They said ladies, don't wear armours for battles,
made me take them off.
I look naked now.
A nihilists' voice thundered in my house.
The breakfast was just some fur
shaved off from anxiety.
I see her crying over her bare skin now.
I wear gowns in winter
to not flaunt my bourbon skin,
but to burn my thoughts scraped on
my body.
The extra flabby fat just swayed along with the
December winds.

Those evenings I stay indoors
because my alcohol is intoxicating for the wolves outside.
Barely escaping death again,
I lay silently on my buttered bed.
There's a Charles Lamb book that I couldn't finish.
As I bled out,
The only thought recurring was,
Why are my hands calling out for help?

10. Hopes

I hope you hold your waist
while you dance in the backyard.
Hoping to compensate for the way
my fingers played with your split ends.
You taught me how pictures change their emotions as time
goes by.
You reeked of love and November.
Smile, so intricately carved yet loosely attached.
Disturbing allocations
with fall, the leaves, the feeling of letting go.
I make excuses to touch your hand,
even a slight grace.
Your fingers were frozen like
you just came home after a rendezvous with winter.
Your thoughts form the shape of a planet,
far away and exist in another time,
so fragile that your coordinates were concealed on the map.
I thought of your chambers as a mark of sanity
and I wouldn't say I liked your adoration for them.
You used to lace them
with fancy words like how my mother drapes her saree.
I disliked how you traced back the circles
I drew on your shrunken shoulders,

as if on a quest to find yourself again.

It was maddening.

I skipped the songs that you slowly hummed to

and built a museum with all the words you'd archived in your

tangled bun.

You travelled to the places that sold dreams.

A manifestation of home and far.

The floor is your haven.

For, you can sink no lower.

11. Human

Not a human,
Blood evaporates every time she cuts open her scars.
She has itching in her palm.
When all she wants to do is hold you in her arms,
And kiss you so lightly.
And her mind scolds her for such hampered thoughts.
She blames her bedridden heart.

I have seen my words make a collage
out of the broken hearts that I had collected.
We were never the same.
The way your hair gushed over your long fingers,
The curve of your lips when someone mentions 'Pink Floyd'.
I was a closeted extrovert
who heard stories of demons gulping down his lovers
because he never knew how to love.

She was the playlist that had everyone on their feet at every
party.
The kind who played the guitar in the school band.
A perfect Swiftee song.
But you were the kind of person
whose songs never made it out of your lips.

I have a novel weaving in my throat,
I know not why death is a teddy that I hug to sleep,
Oh no!
The white crushed pills drowse me out every day,
Do I not see the contradiction.
The medicines help me sleep,
They do not kill the demons,

Screams bottled in those sepia pictures.
A nightmare to relive.
You've held my hand for aeons, now.
To stop me from becoming a monster,
A gene I have in me.

I have a storm in my eyes,
Capturing your essence like the aftermath of wars.
Now let me,
Let me hold your faded skin,
While you paint the stardust.

12. Fear

Someone asked me what fear was
and I did not have an exact answer
but I point to the days
where my blanket could easily pass as my eyes
because the monsters stopped lurking under the bed.
They stopped hiding and started paying rent.
I watch my neighbours sing to themselves while cooking.
Everything looks the same,
but all the songs are permanently linked to saucers of touches.
Fear was inherently manipulated
into a fence that binds my throat
along the lines of my thoughts.
They repeat the question,
I tell them about heights.
The steep high mountains,
spiral stairs
and the feet that never found their place,
the shape of your ear that delicately falls
apart every time I touch.
I show them a tattered piece of a polaroid
taken a day after my first panic attack.
I looked jocund and no one knew about my blistered hands
and the half-cracked window.

What is fear?
Fear neither claimed the front pocket of my luggage,
nor make the weight unbearable.
instead, they closed the curtains on days
light tasted like rust
and watered the plants when I hallucinated
its branches as claws.
The fear of their balding skin
and silver feathers,
moved in with my alter ego.
So now,
fear stays when I have to leave

13. Letters

Insomnia made your cup of coffee.

A bit too strong for my taste,

I watched you flip through the book with some unearthly

sense of fragility.

I cannot read the skin of the people I am in awe of.

You wrote about castles and broken hearts.

The haunted villas that once worshipped Hades now fell

at your feet.

You are graceful like a calm Thursday evening.

write letters, you see.

Talking about the land that got stolen and my complex

drinking habits.

never send them.

They say grief is like a leech.

It never truly leaves.

wondered if you cried to sleep every time you wrote a

love letter.

The bundle of unsent stamps stuck to the tea-dyed

the paper you loved so much has started to rot.

I want to talk about daffodils that remind me of you.

A collection of bipolar thoughts.

grasp onto my pen and hope to the stairs that saw me

whisper to you.

'Patroclus is a rage of passion", we argued till 3 that day and the next day as well.

talk to you about my foster plant 'Kafka' and you bring along yours to keep mine company, naming him Kundera'.

Love is not selfish,

But I believe it is.

I want you to write letters to me about everything melancholic.

Letters addressed to me.

Filled with pictures that smell of cobblestone streets that painted that night.

Salutations of inside jokes and your murder instincts. Selfish.

That is what I have become for you~

The thoughts are infinite like the pages you think you cannot get past.

So, until I can breathe in the rustic air with you,

Write back to me, will you?

—

Love (noun) : /lʌv/

an intense feeling of deep affection ; a great interest and pleasure in something.

14. Warnings

11:00 AM.
You step into my house, watching me make my favourite cup
of tea.
I hear your raspy warning 'give it time.
I hastily drank it and managed to burn my tongue.
Tsch.

2:00 AM.
Your smile starts to choke me and I grip the handle.
Relentless warnings from ma start to crawl around the dark.
I wrap my scaly hands around you.
Guarding you against the demon behind.

4:30 AM.
You shout at my scars instead of whispering.
Pulling hard at the essence of stripping myself dead.
'My thoughts are murderous' you warned.

8:15 AM.
Sometimes I wish you stayed.
Unlike the air that runs every time I unclench my hands.
You didn't seem to be fazed

When the moon glares
through the smokescreen as
I grasped onto the crescent thorn of theirs.
It isn't easy to worship the tiles we fell to.

10:59 AM.
My heart warned me.
My mind shot it.

15. Homebody Stains

Someone once said,

Love loosely so that when it leaves

it does not hurt.

You were always my spring day

and when finally made the deal with the reaper,

You did not tell me.

So, I thought my whole world collapsed.

Everything seemed to move on

And I was at a standstill,

Looking into the pyre,

Trying to make sense of all

The leaks and bleeding from my heart.

Three years later, I still walk around

With the bleeding,

Holding close to everyone I have a

Little bit tight.

My body refuses to see a plumber for all the leaks.

Says it is natural,

That I should grieve.

The leaks have stopped

And on days, if I listen close

I can hear my soul tearing.

Someone once said,
Love loosely so that when it leaves
It does not hurt.
My love comes from the scars that I collected.
My love departs with pain and memories.

16. Metaphors for the night

When I talk about Icarus,

Do not think of the wax stuck wings or the twinkle of excitement in his eyes.

Think of the riddles that pushed him down the window.

When I write about Aphrodite,

Do not think of the charming words and a beautiful face,

Know that scars are never seen in Gods.

When I sing about Hades,

Think of the barren lands that turned our feelings rustic.

The Gods did not know,

Flaws wound them too.

Hearth sat watching the wordless conversations that spun on the vacant thrones.

The trident of destiny was stolen from Poseidon in exchange for a metaphorical love.

She walked through Olympus with pompous strides.

They feared her.

Only her,

She, who learned the tongue of skies.

She hid from them.

For the Gods could not stop shaking the land that clung to their throat.

They wondered how she survived the war.

A war, they fought hard to balance.

An immortal feeling,

A trick that the Gods never knew of.

The goddess of magic only knew how to love.

17. Bedspread

I do not know why,

my heart beats a bit slow

or why

the world seems small to me.

Every godly thing must have a story right?

For me now,

the house next door is the temple that I bow down to.

Why?

Yesterday, a man pronounced dead,

walked in, alive and grateful for life.

The gory details about his accident

that they keep telling me, makes me smile.

Shouldn't it not?

The fact that he fought with Hades piqued my interest.

Millions of questions arose.

If the fight was simple, then why didn't she...

Cry, weep, mourn for her. Write about her. Talk about her.

I hear this every day.

Their little secret schemes to

pull me out of the tight spiderwebs.

Everything I have ever written has all been fictional.

Inspired by the tales of Assef to the quirky wanderer Aza.

I walk out to see the breathing man next door,

struggling to push himself to the veranda.

Death was waiting for him, he said.

Maybe that's why she did not fight.

So, I finally wrote.

I wrote about the man who became my deity.

His 2 AM timetables intrigued me.

His 7:30 call for tea always woke me up until

one day it did not.

That same day, I slept till 12.

My god-fearing grandmother screams into my ear and I wake

up.

Soon, I hear the wailing of the four-wheeler.

My front yard now looks like a 70's film shoot.

The writer's guilt that my main character killed himself

dripped all the words away from me.

I took his life with this ink.

For you, this is just a story.

He is just a fictional character for you.

Someone who just did not make it out of bed this morning.

Hope (noun): /həʊp/

A feeling of expectation and desire for a particular thing to happen

; a feeling of trust.

18. Fossils

i.

The 10-year-old, locked up closet,

now screeched open.

Filled with dust and spider webs with a

ting of selflessness.

Wonderland t'was.

My mother broke the flower vase,

while dusting

and rushed past me,

locking herself,

in the room.

I could hear her fear-ridden cries to

all the garland worn polished images.

Papa, just stood by the door.

Not a word.

He looked at me,

with disgust and remorse.

And the way to Narina,

was then cluttered up with,

unicorn fossils and

records of the Salem Witch trials.

ii.

I had finally bought the 'dream' apartment.

The guilt-ridden female partner,

slowly embraced my parents.

They were glad,

to leave me with a person, they knew.

I was glad,

that there wasn't any need for the covers.

Mother made sure,

all the Gods,

were aligned in a way,

that I would find a prospective groom,

by next Tuesday.

She looked at that

rusty closet,

and told me to break it down,

or never enter her house.

So, I did it.

Burnt down the locked-up life of mine and

kissed my roommate.

Ma ran to cover the images,

and begged me to,

be normal.

Papa,

smiled,

nodded,

promised to take care of ma.

iii.

Two years later,

I hear a familiar voice,

that prayed for me every night,

because

I was scared of ghosts.

This time, it was not to pray,

her voice was sore and husky.

She wanted me to come back,

as the tattooed girl I am,

with my lover of that time.

I walk back in,

to see the unicorn fossils broken

and the records being shredded.

Papa tells me that,

a piece of the,

ruined closet,

now has a special place in ma's drawer.

My home was now welcome to the rainbow-coloured soldiers.

19. Family ties

He lies about the birds that wake him up.
He lies about the burnt toast that he threw in the dumpster.
He lies.
I could feel his lies,
Tightening my breasts.
'He lies, ma'.
Rants to a
Woman who put
Her husband is on a pedestal.
He lies.
He lies about the late-night meetings
That ended up in
Manju Aunty's house.
He lies about the
"preposterous poem recitals"
He'd attended.
But I do not remember
The crooked eyes
Amongst the crowd.

He lies about my freedom
To run away.
'He lies, ma'.

Pedestal, right?
To a world of
Lies,
My mother surrendered.
He lies.
He lies about all the naked pictures
Of 25-year-olds.
He lies about me,
A byproduct of his
Last rendezvous
With my mother.
'he lies, ma'.
Remember the pedestal?
Yes, he's still up there.
He lies.

20. Uncovered hangovers

I saw her,
on a lazy Monday.
My hands were tumbling,
with stories of Hades.
My fingers were covered in,
the royalty of Byron.
I walked past her,
mumbling all the correlation equations.
I hated my exhaustive schedules.

I met her,
This time,
She stole my lips.
The way, she smiled.
sipping on,
white Russian.
Courage was 'brave',
That day.
'Did you know, they add cream
Made from milk powder?'
I was ready to walk back.
Facepalming myself,
Internally.

I noticed her,
This time.
Her face was black with horror.
Halting by the corridors,
Anxious.
Her lips were swollen,
A huge row with,
her potential boyfriend,
I presumed.
I walked on, only stopping
By her side,
gathering myself to,
Ask about yher well-being.
Yet, I stutter for words.
So, my legs fastened their pace,
Blaming my misshapen heart.

I watched her,
Strolling in a pale,
dreary dress.
Wedding of our classmate/
Lavish feast,
Even then,
she looked like a hyena
on a lookout.
She stumbled for words,
Chocolate ice cream,

was probably
the only good thing.
Her tone changed when,
her mother called her.
I was this mere observer,
who was longing,
to be on the
other side
of crystal lies.

I stalked her,
Graduation day.
My sole immunity,
to make this seem non-fictional
'Tejaaaaaaal'
I hear an immortal voice call out,
I turned,
Her waist was hidden by
this better man.
She looked happy,
as she swayed her hips
And reached out for a hug.
The excitement slowly rolled off
as her face met mine.
Small smiles weren't
her thing.
Her eyes told me,

She wanted to run away.
Or was I imagining that?
Maybe,
Just the mild obsession,
toying with my mind.

I disliked her, now.
17 months later.
An email,
A wedding invitation,
'Sourabh
weds
Tejal'.
I realised,
love
was religion
for a few of us.
'Is this for real, Tej?'
I ask and cling onto
the phone
as I hear her mumble,
'I actually don't know what reality is.'

I missed her.
Two years passed
Author of a best seller,
trying to

make sense,

of

social conventions,

created by,

vultures of the North.

She seemed happy

every time,

I sent her my drafts.

But,

this time.

I knew my casual relationship

with reaper,

was pulling

me out.

I call her,

for the last time.

Time, haha.

For me, it was

shadows of melancholy.

Maybe,

This was just a scream for attention,

but I knew she loved

It.

She cried for me.

Today.

I had asked for an open casket.

I could see her,

as she strolled by.

I could almost feel her

dark maroon lips,

on my torn fingers.

I wanted to fight for life

But,

She left.

Now,

I needed to leave.

Did she not know?

I craved for her love even when

I couldn't breathe?

So,

What do you think?

Isn't love and attention the same?

21. Cuckoos

I'm scared of the cuckoos which wake us up every dreary morning.

But I know you hide them on my path.

T'was a Friday evening.

I was crumpled up under the lilac tree, waiting.

Pondering over my unworthy stories.

The belt marks throbbed underneath my burgundy shirt.

I had begun to miss my life on wheels.

Arguments over the millennium.

Starvation for the upper hand.

Undying need for a solemn "okay".

Your hands found my shoulder.

Ignoring the wide-eyed mockers.

Whispered a melody.

Lullabies of the clinched graveyard.

Torn up papers of pain,

conquering the shifting dimensions of,

a 6 feet black hole.

I was constantly telling my unconscious that,

this wasn't love.

Walking away,

from the alcohol stench and unfinished cigars.

Rushing by all the blue mornings.

Brushing off the frivolous taste.

My burnt letters now have a tale to weave.

The vacant path stole my toxic luggage.

And as I strolled on.

The once hidden cuckoos graciously made love to the rolled-
up caterpillars feeding on my soiled heart.

Happiness (noun) : /ˈhapɪnəs/

the state of being happy.

22. Shadow

I see the dark-bodied girl in my lone trips to the wonderland.

She says she mustn't speak of the roads that led her.

I hold her hand.

Every day and every night.

The coldness of her burnt skin balanced with the fire in mine.

I was just a mere toy.

She spoke a language no tongue could ever learn.

Was she a foe of the comfort or an ally of the miseries?

Her hand held mine until the speckled dust dancing through melancholic air washed off her bland tears.

She was a dementor in the land of the muggles.

Tumbling down the stairs, I managed to free myself.

'Please don't be scared.'

She mumbled.

Lying wide awake at 4 a.m.

She told me stories of her yesteryears.

Stories about people whom she loved that left her house with a vacuous bag of bones.

I couldn't bring myself to look in the mirror.

'The sun hides my face and the moon burns my bones.'

She couldn't scream, but all the silent nods that exhausted her soul were crying for help.

She lives beyond my existence.

The meticulous care for the lady in the dark, paved way for the obsession with her grandeur affair with Hades.

This time, I hugged her back.

Calmed the dracarys inside her.

Welcomed the waves that brought her to me.

Thanked the grumbling monsters for the chambers they fostered.

This time, I took her to the mirror.

Ripples of panic rushed in, as I embraced her waist.

The solemn smile matched mine.

I was she.

She was I.

She fit the posture of a lady who never grieved.

'Is this who I will be?'

I asked in desperation.

Her head fell back as she laughed.

Affirming the negative, she said.

'I am who you are not.

Who you chose not to be.

Who you left to die.

I am your redemption from the world you walk on.

The happiness you shout upon. yet I see it not.

If I am wrong.

Tell me,

How healthy is your meal, if sadness is your dessert?'

23. Beast

'Remember the museums that we gazed through?

All the Gobi fry, we stole from the circus stalls.

Remember the beach,

which never failed to bow at our feet?'

The wind in my hair wished me luck. "Enjoy it while you can."

Maybe I was engrossed in my polka dot,

that I paid no heed to those caveats.

Your hands felt the places I knew weren't yours to feel.

You claimed it was purely out of love.

Well, my mother loved you dearly.

The words that left my lips might have told you tales about

how I wasn't afraid of the storm ahead.

Each night I begged my troubled mother to tuck me goodnight.

The monsters under my bed saved me

from the behemoth that was disguised as dad.

My blood ran cold as I watched him gasp for one last breath.

It was a sunny morning that woke me up.

Waved back to the neighbours

whose names I had intentionally forgotten

Wilted leaves smiled as I brushed past their parents.

My bag was replete with scribbled notes
and crushed letters jiggled.
They were mesmerised by the girl
who had killed the masked man.
All the scars had started to heal.
Yet, you could see all the ignored silent screams
and unnoticed tears in my eyes.
All the kids in the pastel shirts whispered within themselves.
"Who was she?"
I made it through the first day.
At least rumours were there to guide me.
The slaves of a force above vowed to never let this overpass
them.
"So, I heard her mom made money by digging on that guy."
Mom?
Even though I took in the air all by myself,
the demons still ruled me.
I looked like the fire on the brink of dying out.
The blood that boiled through my body said
virtue wasn't mine anymore.
Her mom held back the laments,
searching for her lost child.
The salty water drops became my new acquaintance.
The innocent child in me made a tombstone for the
masked man and the soul that he killed.

24. Empty

The valiant space above me rejoiced in your return.

You were an undefeated mortal in the land of Gods.

This was quick.

Your arrival and your departure.

The goblets and ghouls in your head consoled themselves.

They wouldn't come alive now.

I was in awe of you.

The stereotypical bravery never fell under your name.

The dark scared you,

you told me the dark brings

an unusual comfort the light never can.

We were alike.

Every India- Australia cricket match ended with

us nervously pacing the veranda.

Galaxies, Mars and Milky ways in my refrigerator

waited for the clock to strike 8.

We used to rob the universe back then.

The perfectly ruined flowers on the road had a story to tell me.

'All the ruined palaces were once overladen with drops of red

paint that dripped from a severed tongue.'

I remembered you and your mild insanity for those lonely

evening walks,

which were filled with lively banter with the uncle next door.

The tempest was never gone,

hitting me when I was lost and homeless.

You made me believe in souls.

'Souls never die.

They become a part of the sun that glows on you.

Never bury yourself.

It might be just your beloved smiling from above. '

And I cry.

I cry for the soul that will be millions of miles away from home.

Yet, I cannot bid you farewell.

This isn't over yet.

All the promises you made yet never fulfilled

All the first edition books authored by me and inspired by you.

I have a million questions and no one to answer.

The rusty old refrigerator would be filled with confections

if you could walk down the steps of the land of Elysium and help me steal it.

Come down and

tell me how to look through my eyes and

see a better life ahead.

Now, the dark scared me.

The flowers never told me any stories.

The matches never brought me anxiety anymore.

But I know.

That one day I will look up to the Sun.

Not in vain, instead with an endless smile and a heavy heart.
Knowing that the sun never sets on his lover.

25. Catharsis

The brightest stars have stories of a decade to tell you.

The words that leave your fingertips with grace shall never love you the same again.

The moon balanced its judgmental look.

The air had gone bad.

The abhorrent stench of the lifeless bodies lay on the freshly mowed grass.

The line went dead.

The heavy breath left your worm-ridden body for the last time. 'Trick or treat'. The sudden thud on your door woke you from the nightmare.

Stealthily walking down the stairs, you notice the melancholic state of your pet.

You stood there for what seemed like ages.

You couldn't help but stifle a tear.

He seemed lifeless. The blood ran cold and the stiffness of his heart brought you to your senses.

The knock on the door became louder and louder.

Quickening your pace, You rush to the door.

The calendar on your left fluttered in the scattered wind.

It was April.

You slowly take a step back. Looked around.

This neighbourhood has no kids.

The clock struck 3:30.

The rays of warmth and comfort shine through your lavender curtain.
Was it a dream?
Confused as you could be, you contemplate your actions.
How can a man of such intense courage be disarmed by the thought of an unknown entity?
Ashamed, you blame yourself for such irrationality.
Were you scared?
Scared of the hungry soul that was devouring you from inside.
Panic disguised as the courage of immortality, you descended the stairs.
The house seems different.
The picture of you when you were five, building a snowman wasn't there anymore.
The familiar voice of your neighbour w, while he watered the plants every morning, was replaced by stagnant silence.
You take a minute.
You steady your hands.
And you open the door.

You don't know where to look or where to hide.
Is it you or is it the tide?
You look for the answers beneath the skies.
Through wilderness,
you walk the broken fallow land.

You cannot cry,

for your soul believes that it need not confess.

You cannot scream,

for your mouth cares too much for the orphaned.

The paralysed quadruped kept staring at you

as if your body were his.

The scars and wounds on his face,

arms and thighs looked similar to yours.

The perfect child of the Sullens had a below-par existence.

You have heard stories of the demon befriending the mortals.

Is this it?

Is this the demon asking for your beating heart in exchange

for the morbid fascination with the horrors of contemporary

warfare?

You looked down at your marks of survival.

There was no exchange of souls and mortality.

Yet, the demon was still there.

It felt familiar.

His touch and his soothing tone.

The scorching laceration on your palm caught your eye.

You dropped the knife.

We become the demons we destroy.

26. Clarity

She climbed down the walls of shame and humiliation,

a herculean task.

Which crumbled under the one touch of your insanity.

The shadows of light still haunted her.

The monsters hidden behind the veil of darkness waited for

her to surrender.

How can you be a devotee of Durga,

when you trampled her on your way home?

She must have heard you wrong,

definitely.

Because no one would ever find her silence as an answer to

your morbid culture.

Crowd scares her now.

The hundred-year-old man tree which wished her well every

morning and

evening became a blurred memory.

Cigarettes which made love with her broken lips scarred her

body.

You shrugged it off as a mistake, an achievement for your

underlying predator.

She, instead, was trying to make sense of everything that kept

revolving,

like the vulture circling the meat of the fortunate.

Time went by slowly.

"Misfortunes happen every day, Just don't think about it, It will all be fine, We've all been through this."

Bombarded with consolations.

Blaming the beast inside the sorcerer for manipulation.

She gave no acknowledgement.

Numbness left her soul, the minute sun burned her vestal words.

The sullen tears betrayed her.

All the air in the world humbled down to her halo.

Creative (adjective) : /kriːˈeɪtɪv/

relating to or involving the use of the imagination or original ideas
to create something.

27. Letter writing

The torn chappals and the paan stained shirt of yours.

I found solace in them.

The curious Holmes in me wanted to know more.

How you could love the meteors that destroyed an entire civilization.

The way you chose rice soup over all the luxurious food around you.

You told me, you never liked books.

Yet, you knew Byron, Sylvia and Poe like they were your only companions.

We bonded over a bottle of old monk and dog eared diaries.

" I thanked the lucky stars, for that night. "

I caught your eye.

Did I, Jaan?

I was terrible at making conversations.

I was horrible at dates.

Your best friend asked me out for you.

I stumbled for words.

I nodded a half yes.

The next night, our conversations ranged from love to sex to all the movies that we both missed out on.

We became inseparable.

Folklores could not beat the stories that spread about us.

The nights we spent drunk and high, soon became etched in memories.

The balance between weirdness and optimism never worked for us.

I ran away from home.

I heard tattletales of the girl who tore your heart.

But, the bajis were quite distracting.

All the backspaced paragraphs can tell you that ego was at play.

Two years later, I received a phone call.

They told me I was the emergency contact.

' I am calling on behalf of George.'

Was it my fault that I could not recall your name?

I rushed to the hospital with no prior information.

They tell me, you had a minor stroke.

' He asked for you.'

All the balcony stories and the endless marathons of Breakfast at Tiffany's rushed back.

I get hold of my dupatta and walk straight to the chemical-filled dorms.

I smiled, looking at the enormous crowd just sitting by and listening to your fermented stories.

I caught your eye.

You stop talking and slowly walk up to me.

'areh, kya baat hai!'

The hug that followed your Marathi laced Hindi was a mixture of home and wild.

I felt that I could be safe, but I knew that I had to be on the lookout.

We had three years of catching up to do.

You tell me about your wife.

I will tell you about my job.

'mujhe pata tha ki aap hamesha Ek writer honge.'

The carefree bache of the 90s would never forgive the awkward silence between us.

You told me about all the cities you travelled to and all the people you met.

'Did you miss me, Jaan?'

I whimpered a no.

A simple smile, as if you knew the answer all along.

Then you spoke with such certainty,

'Don't worry, Sooraj Mukhi.

The lord of the sky can never make up for the meticulous mistakes.

The lord of the sea rushes by you, ignoring the loud yet silent screams.

The lord of war cannot apprehend your survival scars.

And the lord of the underworld lives in awe of you. '

Listening to you use the references of my favourite mythology, was my last stray of strength.

'This is it, my love.

I got my last wish.'

I have lost people over and over, but nothing has made me anathematize Lord Yama.

I went back, with a heavy heart.

Sleepless nights found me again.

I was a soul seeking vengeance on an unknown.

The news of your departure reached me soon enough.

With a strong mind and an exhausted heart.

I bid you farewell.

I was asked to give a eulogy.

What was I to say?

Goodbye?

But, George. You never left me.

In every nightmare that keeps me awake, I think of you.

In every death I hear about, I think of you.

I think of you in all good and bad, George.

All I ask is,

When can I see you?

28. Story for Santa

Dear Santa,

I remember the white beard and the merry laughter.

It was the only happy memory that kept ringing all along.

But now, the merry laughter is a feeble voice amongst the helpless cries.

I remember the heart bigger than the tummy, filled with stories of the joyous past.

When you asked me if I was a good child.

I whispered yes.

I kept quiet when mockery hit me.

I stood my stand when I was scaled for scoring less.

I didn't shed a tear when my heart took a fall.

I hoped that I made you proud.

You glanced at me, before asking what I wanted for Christmas.

All of a sudden I was lost.

Mend my heart?

Bring back my family?

Lost childhood?

I had a battle of questions inside my head.

Sensing my apprehension, you smiled at me and said, 'You will find your ground.'

The lores of how Santa brings gifts and sweets for all the good
children never appealed to me.
The kids had told me that you make their wishes come true.
I had no materialistic attachment.
I didn't make it back in time to tell you what I wanted.
My mom said you had to go make other kids happy.
I wondered how you did that.
Happiness was a cultivated feeling that forgot to sow in me.
I kept my ground, searching for the seed that flew away.
Twenty years later, I still go back every year, hoping to reunite
with myself.
So, this is a 20-year-old who keeps waiting to put out cookies
and milk every year.
Hoping.
Begging
Praying
That you'll bring the happiness that I lost.

29. Tales

I tell pa to begin again.
To tell me about,
all the machos in their love stories.
How Ma ran towards him with daffodils just wavering.
He laughs at my generic love story.
This was his favourite fairytale,
and my ultimate love goal.
The 1970s was a miserable time for Ma.
The Beatles were disbanded,
The emergency period was a bracelet for their love capsule.
He stops mid-way
and asks me if she ever thought of marrying him.
This was their inside joke.
I tell Pa to begin again.
This time the story is a bit different.
He forgets ma's name,
he makes up for the latter by cracking a limerick.
Then I wonder, if theirs were the love story,
I wanted to live in.
I pour him, his two shots of whiskey,
He said ma could weave poems out of his drink.
He finishes it in a gulp.
The guilt-ridden look,

his trembling fingers,
the droopy eyes,
they were the heroes in my adrak chai.
Pa says he heard the doorbell,
I walk out of his room,
glancing at the blue blanket drapped
over my mother.
The guests had brought friends,
Pity and sympathy.
But I didn't know why?

I go back to Pa
and urge him to begin again.
Only this time, it was a confession.
He said he wanted to be the wind that never slowed.
So, he ran where his scars took him.
Hid where his blood ran muddy,
And killed when his eyes grew dark.
He came back,
with a hand to write and a foot to run.
He came back,
when the poetess had destroyed herself in a whirl of suitors at
night.
He said he craved her
when the couch had space.
He wanted a new story,
A love story, he was in.

So, begin again Pa.

I said,

and succumbed to his dominant tongue.

• 87 •

30. Comfort

This was comfort for me
until you left me shattered in ways
only the sky could understand.
I waited for the stars to burn out,
for ours was a love that could
never exceed the walls which I built safely around the
cigarettes and the 3 AM conversations.
I'm holding onto every part of me
that believed in man-made stories
of her prince charming.
I'm holding onto the whispers,
I've grown used to
when you think I'm asleep.
I'm holding onto every colour
I've used to paint
a picture, so blurred
that you laughed at it.
I'm holding onto
You,
You, who wished for a fairytale
but got a goddess with broken wings.
You, who seemed to wander with the wilderness,
turned into a home for a lost wisp.

You, who started giving into,
a lie you were hiding behind.
And I'm still here,
holding onto your shadow
with my,
scarfed fingers,
struggling to let go.

—

Memory (noun) : /ˈmɛm(ə)ri/

the faculty by which the mind stores and remembers information ;

the length of time over which a person or event continues to be

remembered.

31. Reasons

I cannot recall all the reasons,
why I fell out of love.
The 12 AM calls when you are slightly drunk
And playing xbox with your mates.
You would still call to tell me about how Rohan made
sandwich with bread and kheer.
I giggle a little, while you whisper into the metallic device of
how you miss tugging my drenched curls.
Maybe, it is the 2 PM video calls when you are in class and I
ignore cause,
I was busy watching the re runs of a new show I just found.
You don't tell me how your day went,
And I never bothered to ask.
We meet up every weekend and laze around in a bookstore.
Were we afraid to talk to each other, or were we just enjoying
the silence that made home between us?
I watch you from the corner of my eyes as I take a long drag
from my cigarette.
I notice how your hair was now brown and that you changed
your glasses.
You stopped wearing your mother's ring around your neck, it
now gracefully hugged your finger.

I remembered the nights, you used to wake up screaming,

How I used to calm you down, like a lost star in a forest of embers.

I cannot recall all the reasons

Why I fell out of love,

A bundle of letters lay on my couch unread.

Maybe, you write too much.

Your feelings all pushed down in a paper that I never picked up.

I pick up an alphabet which you plucked from the first typewriter you owned.

I realise that it was among a bunch of other things that you gifted me.

Other things.

You had saved the napkin on which we played tic tac toe while listening to ABBA.

The X's had started to fade away.

And the dried flowers from our first trip to Ladakh which I had forgotten to keep inside my diary.

Everything seemed out of place.

I cannot recall all the reasons,

Why I fell out of love.

I watched the trees on our way back home that night,

Nodding lightly to me as if they understood my pain.

I stand outside my house,

I bid a small goodbye and wish you the best.

As I watch you drive away,

I rush to my balcony, hoping for the leaves to hug me tight.
I cry and cry into the night,
Realising,
I cannot recall all the reasons,
Why I fell out of love.

32. Guilt

They talked about you in metaphors and
wondered why I fell in love.
I was the kind who gushed about
the Lilies that grew on the Sunflower fields.
The kind you wouldn't think twice
before running over.
My therapist asked me why I write
and I tell her about you.
She had an order with her patients
but I did not have an order for my answers.
Just a plain, 'yes' or a 'no'.
I have watched your fingers trying to make a poem
unromantic by adding your raw touches.
I finally found your obsession for
love letters and
took on the role to finish your tales.
For loving you was like finishing off a book,
Drowning in the familiar pang of guilt.

I didn't wish on the falling stars,
hoping you'd come back.
Even though,
I missed your fingers lacing the ice tea latte and

highlighting Inferno.
Wanting to see that thunder in your eyes,
the one that you stole from Olympus.
Playing with your hair,
while you contemplate on a better chai place.
I never wished on a falling star
before I met you.
Pity.
Now, wishing on a sun who woke me up every morning,
made more sense than
a star whose 'hope' never showed up.

33. Rants

-

Restless rants.

Tragically beautiful verses.

Significant other halves.

I ran away from her wide heart and childish memories.

Every night,

I hear the blackened vessels being thrown down. 'Mere idiots'.

I hear my father shout with his authoritative melody.

I snuck under my torn mattresses.

I was his next interest.

My Mondays were filled with bottles

That covered up my bluish black

Marks of silent screams.

Next week,

It would be my tennis elbow, 'I slipped.' Would be my only

answer.

I knew how to hide from him

Or strike back.

But he was always stronger than me.

So, last night

I stole the keys from Aachi's drawer
And l locked myself up.
Maybe,
He was really good at hide and seek

Or maybe

My uncontrollable muffles sobs were like music to his ears.
He screamed his past through my eyes.
The stains of every hug and comfort left on my skin.
I rushed out into the same world that engraves in every
unturned stone about this man.
I smile through my chapped lips that ache from muttering the
name of a lover that never walked down.

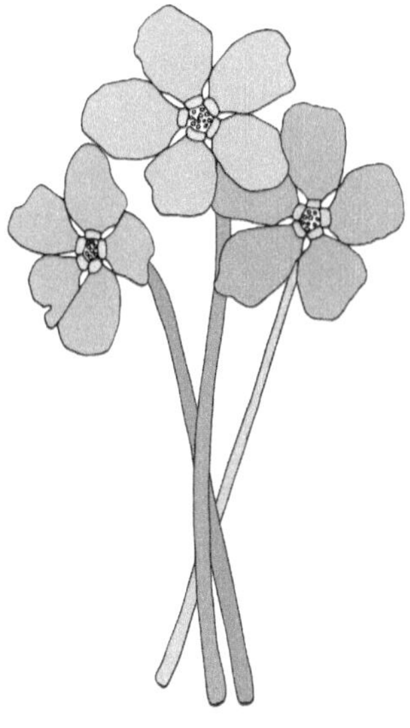

Comfort (noun) : /ˈkʌmfət/

the easing or alleviation of a person's feelings of grief or distress. ; a warm quilt

34. Monsters

You watch me topple down all the pins at the alley.

A wacky grin under your mushed over hair and I was climbing stars.

Nothing could go wrong.

Before you,

I was the girl who never spent her evenings wondering why no glass slippers arrived at her door.

I used to come home to a deadly silence which sold nightmares to my void brain.

I would watch you sleep and wonder who told you fairy tales that slayed the demons in your tongue.

You said,

spring was done and walked away with the sweaters.

I stopped wondering why we swallow the burning stars.

Quickly realising that we gulp down our sober self for every lingering touch.

Winter came late,

So did the snow.

Yet, I see a man on the other side with fire in his eyes.

You digged your way onto the land that never stopped blooming,

for mine was filled with ravens and creatures hidden under the sun.

The man on the edge welcomed you with the very warmth
from my broken words.

This isn't wrong,

is what you told me,

before you tamed my monsters and called them your own.

- excerpts from a poem I left for the flames.

35. Pages from my thought

-+• I wondered what sights my windows held.
But, none of them told me bed tales,
like the broken brick walls did.
She is the beast,
who tore through all stories with
a steel heart.
For her, art was not to fail.
Watching as the palace broke down
for her to grow.
She is the beast,
not with fury hair or
sharpened claws.
She is the beast whose
fairytale got lost within herself.

• I write about the skies.
And you speak in a tongue
only the stars could nod off to.
The world became barren with
your illusions.
Falling in love.
Your illusions took up a form.
This 10 year old form,

changed according to consequences.
I stole glances at the poems
you wrote on napkins.
You eyes stare at me,
as if I were a foreign tongue
which screamed for a story,
that now sends a shiver
down my spine.
You watch people,
from a distance,
as they speak.
As if even a sullen whimper could
burn your body.
Falling in love.
A mirage.
Is it not,
a bedtime story for the ghosts?
Is it not,
a lie that trembles beyond your eternal skies?
I break down the symmetrical walls
and tell you why I write.
3 years back,
you left because I write about the stars
I never saw.
So, now,
I write about the moon
who vanquished your sky.

• I cannot pen down my thoughts.
It gets carved on my legs.
There are stains on my white shirt.
tho I used the popular detergent brand.
I do not know the shape of my heart,
so I draw a bottle.
The house is silent,
Blood everywhere.
Sad premises, I grew up here.
The memories are tainted but
the sepia etched sounds
are written down under my chin.

36. Tears (TW: Death)

My tears take the form of a goddess I never prayed to.
But now-
I hoped for a life less killed.
Empty chest and hollow hugs, touch that fornicates under the friction of two smiles.

Why do you lament,
When you know the joys of a dystopian era
A world which hid their abuse,
By painting sunsets and skyscrapers every other day.
And I cry.
My tears flow into the river that once buried your laughter.

I saw the sky today,
White and like a shroud that seems stuck on the wind's body.
And I lay like a corpse because feeling anything
seemed too technical

I watch my plants grow a little everyday.
They lean towards the sun and so I named them after the moon.
My sore body understands my Grandmother's smudged tear droplets.

I have been taught to pay heed to casualties, ignore maladies.

Desires started to rot,
The smell unheaved a series of memories,
Which the crushed soil knew better.
Earth paused for a while,
Stagnant and bloody,
Lying on (ni) hill (ism)
I will stay in the lonely house,
Wandering,
Hoping,
For even a stuffed man as companion.

Everything seems a bit simple today,
And more ridiculous tomorrow.
Death seemed to be tired of her evergrowing collection.
I dare not breathe without counting.
Breathe without whispering a thank you into the universe.
For the people who vanished, I am the plague.

37. Drought

It always made sense to me.
Writing about the people
we've lost.
It's like a state of being.

Dadi was a great storyteller.
She used to lure me to bed
with the Rakshasas and
the cruel kings.
She wakes up at 5
in the morning,
cleans the house,
makes chai for all the 10 members
and then comes to wake me up.
'Only if you wake up in the morning,
can you see the birds following the wind?
It's a way of life, Pappu.'
Knowing that I was her favourite,
I used to play the puppy dog face card and
win every time.

Every summer vacation was spent
at her place trying to fish,

how to pluck ripe mangoes or
learn how to unscrew the bolts from the doors
and every vacation used to end up
with my tantrums of
how I hated it back in the town.
I used to wave goodbyes
as tears trickled down my face.

One day,
I asked her about my father.
It was rare for me to bring up
his name and
even more strange hearing
her say it.
As though,
if she uttered his name louder,
it would fall off her tongue.
As if,
every memory and illusion
she had
would slowly disintegrate
into reality
She told me how I was exactly like him
but a bit more mischievous.
Dadi asked if I remembered his face.
Papa had passed away
when I was 4,

the only memory I have of him and ma
together
was when she used to hug his picture and
cry for hours long.
I did not tell Dadi about the hazy memory.

Papa was excited to have a baby girl.
He started taking out ma for dinner
every day and later to a play.
He loved poetry.
He used to sit on the veranda
early morning
and recite poems like
a conversation.
It just flowed out of him.
Soon, ma went into labour
and papa was at work.
He rushed to the hospital to hear
that it was a
stillborn.
Dadi wipes away her tear,
as she continues.
Losing a child broke my
papa's heart.
He stopped writing poetry.
He got slacked from work due
to his complete ignorance.

He started drinking.
His drinking later took the form of
abuse on my mother.
He blamed her for his daughter's death and
every morning,
he apologised.

Years later,
when I was born.
Dada was working in a new company.
He did not bother to pick up
Dadi's calls.
He came home in the evening to
see a crib,
he peeks into it
and sees a baby girl looking at him
amused.
She said,
He named me Mira after
his favourite poet,
Mirabai.

When I was 5,
I wake up hearing mama crying.
Dada had passed away.
It was a silent attack.
I remember wondering,

where my evening lollipops went.

It's been 10 years since.
I never cried for him.
Every morning,
I would walk to the veranda,
but it seemed as if that place had
an unknown vengeance
towards me.
The scorching sun or
the buzzy mosquitoes
never let me sit there.

Later that summer,
as I go back home.
I hear mama complaining
about the droughts that had started off
in the nearby town.
Our village would be dead soon,
if it does not rain.
I paid no heed to it
as I rush to the almirah in
mama's room.
It opens with a creak and
as I peek in.
I see books with fancy cars and
coloured horses,

in the corner was a small notebook in which

he wrote his daily routines.

I flip through the pages to

June 14th, 2005.

I see a blank page.

Disheartened,

I look to the next page to see

a few sentences,

" The fingers I held today,

grasped mine.

She was laughing as I looked at

her."

I turned to the page,

he wrote before he died.

" Mira amuses me every time with

a new thing.

she is curious about all things.

Haha.

Ever heard of a father looking up to

his daughter?'

This was followed by a poem he wrote,

which went in length about

his adoration for me.

I broke down,

on the floor,

listening to my heartbeat

weaken

with each sob I muffled.

I rush back to the Veranda,
his favourite place.
It now welcomed me with
the cold wind that brought the rain.

Gentle (adjective) : /ˈdʒɛnt(ə)l/

having or showing a mild, kind, or tender temperament or

character.

38. Fragmented memory

I fell in love.
Not the way,
You weaved your arms
Around me
But the way your eyes
Screamed for another story.

A story that now sends
a shiver down
your daughter's throat.
You watch the passerby
with such casualty.
As if one touch
from them would
burn your
immortal soul.

I write at night
when the words turn to gin and tonic.
I write at night
because the sky is blank
and
my vision gets blurry.

I tell her about my obsession
with love letter
and how I have one painted on my
feet.
Love that walks with me,
to people,
I could not
measure with my
heart.

She points to the red-haired human.
who pushes past me
every day.
Their hands are silver
and their feet are always hidden.
I see the paintbrushes
which peek at me
through his half-torn bag.

Half smile and a wave
led to us sneaking out
at night
to eat ice cream out of the tub.
writing letters on our skin.
crossing borders and
checkpoints for

warmth.
A connection,
that Cadence pushed away
but never forgot.

I fell in love with the red-haired human.
Who,
disappeared after the sunset.
Taking with them,
my words and silence.

Now,
My body is painted blue and
It reminds me of someone,
I cannot remember.

39. Imaginations

Midnight

I cannot be bothered by the knives
that stabbed me in the back.
The world stands on
the bilateral illusions agenda.
The metaphorical scriptures guarantee
Immunity for the thrones.
Who am I?
Only an enthused darkness,
Shaped by the
Cages of power.
A distorted creature from
the rat race.

Dawn

Is it magic?
To feel like you are dying
and living at the same time?
Is it love?
When you cannot love
the collapsed

thoughts of meticulous
stories that flow in
me.

The deep valley of insecurity
filled up the land of
blissfully patient
memories.
The abyss ran into
the darkness,
that was looked after by
Hades.
Naked, collapsed Olympus
waited for the wilted
Lilies.
The mountains that I climbed
showed me how to breathe
without dying.
I never realised,
how I dreamt of
a barren land
and climbed the
highest peak.

Noon.

Have you not seen,
the comfortable smile of the
waker of this land?
exactly when he sees
his beloved down amidst
the uncanny group.
Does he know?
Does he know of the
wounded rhymes she sings,
while watching him relocate without
exception?
The drooping head of his,
makes the tranquil imagine
how the sunflowers can
never yearn for
the angry, monstrous big pellet
of fire
The fire,
who never heeds to his succumbed
cries.
Yet, they never watch the
woebegone lights of
the crucified sun.

40. Warmth

Warmth (noun): /wɔːmθ/

The quality, state or sensation of being warm; moderate heat.
Enthusiasm, affection or kindness.

The scribbles on my hands as we watch the sunset. You point out the coldness in the air, tangling the earphones once again and I slowly nod a 'yes' and now every time I hear sirens, I am reminded of the ocean that held me after you faded away.

How do I write when all the words are stuck between my shoulder blades? My heels barely touch the ground while I watch anxiety knit a quilt and tie me at the end of it. It is comfort or maybe kindness. I soon learned to equate her with safety.

The compass stopped working after I moved into my father's house. I did not get it fixed as I heard him mumble a short 'love you'. So I stayed directionless and built a house for us in the void.

I watched the skies through my partner's eyes. The clouds kept shivering and the vision got too blurry, so I held their hands and drew patterns. I kept their shrivelled fingers dry throughout the storm.

I see people in colours and numbers in shapes. I know Rectangle is 11 and Yellow Ochre is Swathi. There are times when the colours and shapes start to crumble, memories fade or North becomes unemployed. Religiously, I would turn off the lights.

Warmth is a habit that I keep grasping onto.
It is my dessert after every scream.

41. Love

We are all illusions built from a phoenix.

A kind of tale they are afraid to whisper.

I was 9 when my grandfather told me that girls should not be loud.

I nodded, maybe it is the fear on his stone-cold face.

So, at the age of 11, I fell for a man

Who had a fire like hair.

He painted the walls at night,

Skipped classes like he owned the college and held me soft.

At 11, I was completely romanticised by the thought of 'love',

I never knew that he planned on crushing my immortal soul soon.

At 13, he left me for a woman who had fluttery eyes and a tongue like a snake.

So now,

I thought love was like a chameleon that could change shapes and colours.

She caught my eye on the verge of my adulthood.

A girl who always wore jhumkas with such resounding confidence.

On our first date, I asked her favourite colour and she said blue but how it is never constant.

That night I dyed my hair blue.

Three months later,

She whispered into my ears that she loves me while we were watching Grey's.

I looked at her with surprise,

Not knowing the complete meaning.

Her eyes waited for my response as I kissed the top of her head and murmured an

illegible yes.

But, I do not think I meant that.

Soon, I heard my teacher claim with all her life that love is a fallacy.

And I thought her to be right.

It was all a lie.

A lie that was blatantly fed to us.

I went back home and reread the poems of Keats and Yeats.

The word kept screaming in my ears, a mere attempt to disappear.

At the age of 21, I slept with a woman who never believed in love.

She used to play with my hair,

But never bothered to talk to me.

And I think,

I loved the morbid silence between us.

For me, now, that was love.

Three months later, I stand at her engagement hearing her vow that she only

loved them.

Only them.

I grew up in a household that was torn apart by this vicious feeling called love.

I grew up knowing that love never stays.

At the age of 24, I started loving expiry dates.

You, metaphors, scars, poems and the moon.

I fell for you after years of contemplation.

You were like those sweet mangoes on a summer evening.

Childish, I know.

You were like a house in the dark,

With goblins and dragons lurking around.

.

You were a poem that was never scared of being retold.

And me,

A poem waiting to be finished.

So, I left.

I left behind the world where I always ended up tightening my grip on your neck

while I dragged you back home.

I left because the stars that brought us together had burnt to embers.

Not long after, you found someone who carried the moon on their palms.

I was broken but still fascinated by the walls that I started building around me.

This is my story.

The story of why I leave.

But now, I hope I will stay without an expiry date for you.

Cause,

Letting go is easy.

Loving is not

Emotions (noun) : /ɪˈməʊʃ(ə)n/

a strong feeling deriving from one's circumstances, mood, or
relationships with others and oneself.

About The Author

Neha Ann Jishnu (Skye/Blue) goes by the pronouns They/Them. They are pursuing Masters in English at Jyoti Nivas College. They are an occasional poet, avid reader, Connoisseur of chai, art and a romanticised observer. They can often be seen at bookstores finding Ishiguro or Ocean Vuong. Writing is how they survive in this world, how they can assimilate into life.

A Note From Neha

It is okay, sometimes just breathing is enough.

Yours truly.